A GAME OF FUNCTIONS

A GAME OF FUNCTIONS

ROBERT FROMAN

ILLUSTRATED BY ENRICO ARNO

THOMAS Y. CROWELL COMPANY · NEW YORK

YOUNG MATH BOOKS

Edited by Dr. Max Beberman, Director of the Committee on School Mathematics Projects, University of Illinois

BIGGER AND SMALLER *by Robert Froman*

CIRCLES *by Mindel and Harry Sitomer*

COMPUTERS *by Jane Jonas Srivastava*

THE ELLIPSE *by Mannis Charosh*

ESTIMATION *by Charles F. Linn*

FRACTIONS ARE PARTS OF THINGS
by J. Richard Dennis

GRAPH GAMES *by Frédérique and Papy*

LINES, SEGMENTS, POLYGONS
by Mindel and Harry Sitomer

LONG, SHORT, HIGH, LOW, THIN, WIDE
by James T. Fey

MATHEMATICAL GAMES FOR ONE OR TWO
by Mannis Charosh

ODDS AND EVENS *by Thomas C. O'Brien*

PROBABILITY *by Charles F. Linn*

RIGHT ANGLES: PAPER-FOLDING GEOMETRY
by Jo Phillips

RUBBER BANDS, BASEBALLS AND DOUGHNUTS:
A BOOK ABOUT TOPOLOGY *by Robert Froman*

STRAIGHT LINES, PARALLEL LINES,
PERPENDICULAR LINES *by Mannis Charosh*

WEIGHING & BALANCING *by Jane Jonas Srivastava*

WHAT IS SYMMETRY? *by Mindel and Harry Sitomer*

Edited by Dorothy Bloomfield, Mathematics Specialist, Bank Street College of Education

AREA *by Jane Jonas Srivastava*

GAME OF FUNCTIONS *by Robert Froman*

LESS THAN NOTHING IS REALLY SOMETHING
by Robert Froman

NUMBER IDEAS THROUGH PICTURES
by Mannis Charosh

SHADOW GEOMETRY *by Daphne Harwood Trivett*

SPIRALS *by Mindel and Harry Sitomer*

STATISTICS *by Jane Jonas Srivastava*

VENN DIAGRAMS *by Robert Froman*

Library of Congress Cataloging in Publication Data. Froman, Robert, date. The game of functions. (A Young Math Book) SUMMARY: Gives directions for a game which demonstrates the basic principles of functions and graphs. 1. Functions—Juv. lit. 2. Graphic methods—Juv. lit. [1. Functions. 2. Graphic methods] I. Arno, Enrico, illus. II Title. QA331.3.F76 515 74-2266 ISBN 0-690-00544-X ISBN 0-690-00545-8 (lib. bdg.)

1   2   3   4   5   6   7   8   9   10

A GAME OF FUNCTIONS

YOUNG MATH BOOKS

Have you noticed how some things depend on other things?

Suppose you wake up on a summer morning. It's a beautiful day with no clouds in the sky and no wind. You have a great idea.

"Mother," you say, "Mother, can we have a picnic this afternoon?"

She smiles and looks out the window.

"Yes," she says, "if the weather stays as nice as this. But only if it stays nice. If it gets cloudy or windy, we will go shopping and buy you some shoes."

This means that what you will do in the afternoon depends on the weather.

1

Nice weather means
you will have a picnic.

Bad weather means
you will go shopping.

Or you could say that what you will do in the afternoon is a FUNCTION of the weather. Once you know the afternoon weather, you know what you will do.

Of course, something unexpected might happen—say, somebody might get sick—which would stop the picnic even in nice weather. But here we will say that nothing of this sort does happen.

Can you think of other kinds of things that depend on something else?

How about the length of time it takes you to go around the outside of your house?

The length of time it takes you to go around depends on how you go.

It takes a long time if you crawl.
It takes less time if you walk.
It takes still less time if you run.

5

You can say it with pictures like this:

How you go

means — a long time

means — less time

means — still less time

How long it takes

How long it takes to go around the house is a function of how you go.

Can you think of other sorts of functions?

What about feeling hungry? Is it a function of anything?

How hungry you feel usually depends on how long it has been since you ate a meal. Right after a good breakfast you don't feel hungry at all. A couple of hours later you may want a snack. Four hours after breakfast you probably will be very hungry for your lunch.

What about how far you can see? Can it be a function of anything?

If you have good eyes or glasses that help you see well, how far you can see is a function of how clear the air is.

In a dense fog you can see only a few feet.
On a rainy day you can see a lot farther.
In clear weather you can see a long way.

Some kinds of functions are more exact than this.

If you want to mail a letter that weighs one ounce or less, you put one regular stamp on the envelope. Of course you can also use any stamps whose cost adds up to the same amount as a regular stamp. But we are using only regular stamps.

If the letter weighs between one ounce and two ounces, you use two stamps.

If the letter weighs between two and three ounces, you use three stamps.

The number of stamps you use is a function of the weight of the letter.

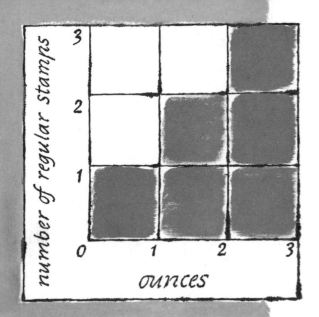

At the post office there is a chart that shows how many stamps you need for letters of different weights. But you can make your own chart or graph.

This really is a graph of the number of stamps needed for letters mailed only to places in this country or Canada. If you want the letter to go by ordinary mail, you use one kind of stamp. If you want it to go by air mail, you use another kind of stamp.

But if you want to send a letter by air mail to someplace overseas, this graph does not tell you what you need to know. For overseas air mail you must use one stamp for the first *half* ounce, two stamps for over one-half ounce up to one ounce, and three stamps for over one ounce up to one and one-half ounces. For each half ounce you add, you must add a stamp.

Your graph of stamps needed for overseas air mail would look like this.

A graph is a way of showing how one thing is a function of another. These two graphs show how the number of stamps needed is a function of the weight of a letter.

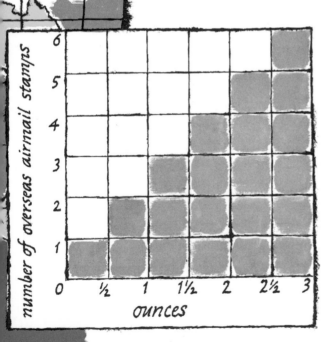

There is a game
you can play called
"A Game of Functions."
It's a little like the
game called "May I?"
That's the one in which
the person who is "it"
tells you to take a
certain number of steps
in one direction.
Then you have to say
"May I?" before you
take the steps.

In "A Game of Functions" you don't just take steps. You can make any kinds of moves you want to. You don't have to wait to be told to make them, and you don't have to ask permission.

Instead, you decide for yourself that every time you make a certain number of moves in one direction you will next make a certain number of the same moves or other ones in another direction.

You can make a graph when you play this game, too. It will be an outdoor graph. Just find in your yard or somewhere nearby a big, flat, open place where you can make marks in the ground. Or if you can't scratch the ground, get sticks or stones to put down for marks. If you play on pavement, use chalk or stones for marks.

Start at one corner of the open space. Make a line with your heel along one side of the space or use a row of sticks or stones. Go back to your starting place and make another line along the other side.

Now it's time for you to decide. You are going to begin at the corner and make a certain number of certain kinds of moves out along one of your lines. Each time you do this you will make a certain number of certain other moves up into the open space.

Suppose you decide to start with a simple function. The moves you make will be steps. And for each step you take out, you will take one step up into the open space.

You go to the corner and take one step out along the line. Then you turn and take one step up into the open space. You mark the place where you wind up by scratching a big X on the ground or by putting down a stick or stone.

You go back to the corner and take two steps out. This means that you must take two steps up into the open space. Again, you mark the place where you stop.

You go back to the corner and take three steps out. Now you take three steps up into the open space and mark your place.

This first outdoor graph looks a little like the graphs of how the number of stamps needed is a function of the weight of the letter. The marks you have made are in a row slanting up to the right like the dark squares in the stamps graphs.

This is a very simple kind of function. It's more fun to make up more complicated functions. Can you think of one?

How about taking three steps out and then only one step up into the open space?

How many steps up would you take after nine steps out?

How many steps up after fifteen steps out?

Here is how your outdoor graph of this function will look if you mark the place where you stop at the end of each of your series of moves up:

up

out

But steps are not the only moves you can make. You also can hop on one foot.

Or you can skip from one foot to the other.

Or you can jump with both feet together.

You might decide to take a skip and a jump up
into the open space every time you take a hop out.
How many skips and how many jumps will you
make up after three hops out?

Remember: You can make up any ways of moving you like. Then decide how many moves of which kinds you will make along the bottom line before making a certain number of moves of other kinds up into the open space.

Another way to play "A Game of Functions" is on paper. Find some graph paper if you can.

Or make your own graph paper with a ruler. Then number the lines Out and the lines Up.

Now, what shall the function be? You might decide that for an easy starter you will go one square Up for every two squares Out.

How many squares Up after six squares Out?

How many squares Up after twenty squares Out?

If you mark the place where you stop after each move Up, you will make a graph of the function. And when you make a graph on paper, you can draw a line through your marks.

UP

Does this line tell you anything interesting?
Can you learn from it how many squares Up
after one square Out? After five squares Out?
After thirty squares Out?

OUT ⇨

28

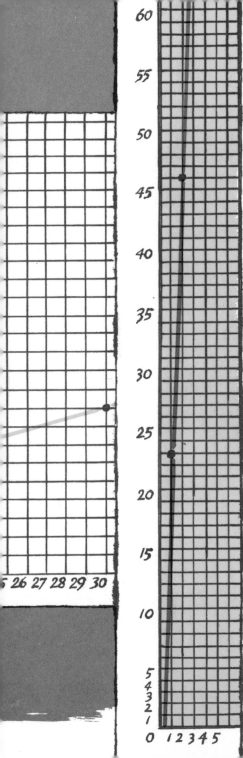

It's fun to make up
more complicated functions
on paper, too.

How about five squares Up
after four squares Out?

Or three squares Up
after ten squares Out?

Or twenty-three squares Up
after one square Out?

If you would like to make a graph of a really complicated function, try the rule that every time you go Out a certain number of squares you must go Up that number *times* itself.

This means that if you go Out one square you go Up one times one—which is one.

If you go Out two squares, you go Up two times two— which is four.

If you go Out three squares, you go Up three times three— which is nine.

How many Up after four Out? After five? Six?

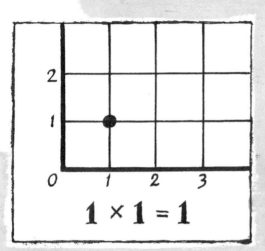

$1 \times 1 = 1$

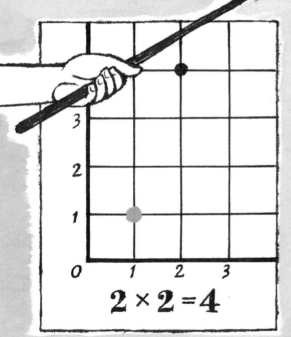

$2 \times 2 = 4$

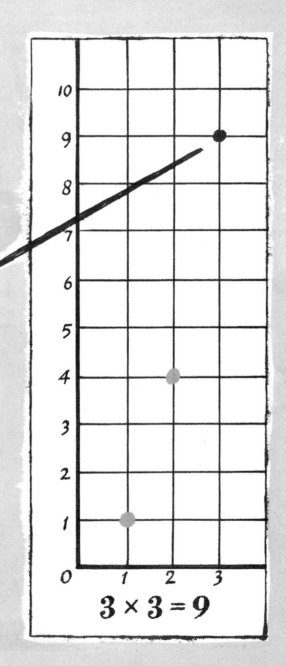

$3 \times 3 = 9$

31

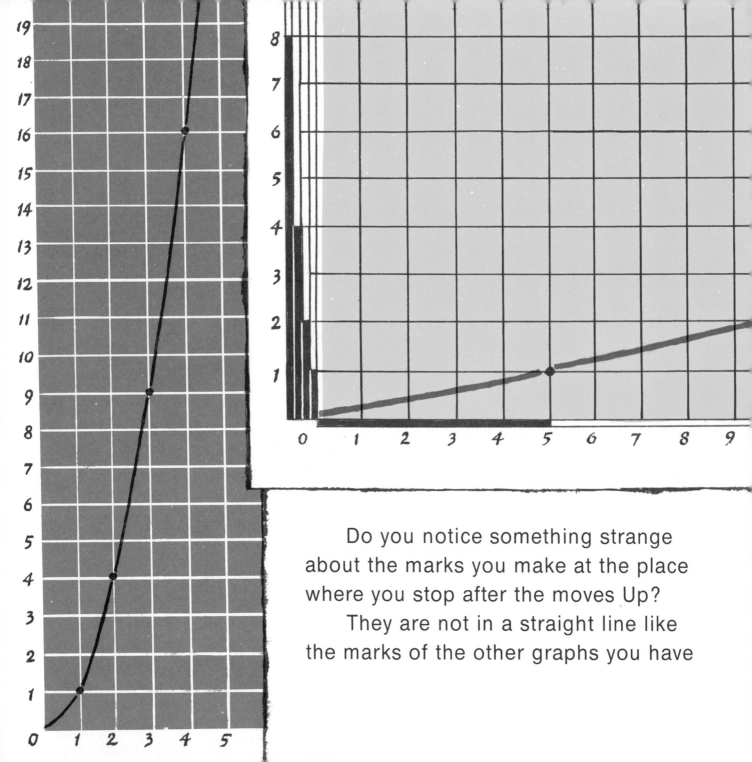

Do you notice something strange about the marks you make at the place where you stop after the moves Up?

They are not in a straight line like the marks of the other graphs you have

12　13　14　15　16　17　18　19　20　21　　25　26　27

made. The line that connects these
marks is a curve.

Try to think up some other
complicated functions and make
graphs of them.

ABOUT THE AUTHOR

This is Robert Froman's fifth book for the Young Math series. He says, "I always wanted to be a writer, and I had the luck to discover when I was a child that mathematics could be exciting, too. I like to pass that discovery along. The books I've done for the Young Math series are my favorite way of accomplishing this. What I've been trying to do in them is to make some of the basic ideas of mathematics both meaningful and intriguing to young readers."

Mr. Froman and his wife Elizabeth Hull Froman, who is also an author of children's books, live in Tomkins Cove, New York.

ABOUT THE ILLUSTRATOR

Enrico Arno has had a distinguished career as an illustrator of children's books. He was born in Mannheim, Germany, and educated in Berlin. In 1940 he emigrated to Italy, where he worked for book publishers in Milan and later in Rome. Mr. Arno came to the United States in 1947. He and his wife live in Sea Cliff, New York.